DATE DUE

Great African Americans

Booker T. Washington

Leader and educator

Revised Edition

Patricia and Fredrick McKissack

Series Consultant
Dr. Russell L. Adams, Chairman
Department of Afro-American Studies, Howard University

Enslow Publishers, Inc.

40 Industrial Road	PO Box 38
Box 398	Aldershot
Berkeley Heights, NJ 07922	Hants GU12 6BP
USA	UK

http://www.enslow.com

To Estelle and Mike Smith, Happy Memories

Revised edition of Booker T. Washington: Leader and Educator © 1992

Library of Congress Cataloging-in-Publication Data

McKissack, Pat, 1944–
  Booker T. Washington : leader and educator / Patricia and Fredrick McKissack.—Rev. ed.
    p. cm. — (Great African American series)
Includes bibliographical references and index.
  ISBN 0-7660-1679-X
  1. Washington, Booker T., 1856–1915—Juvenile literature. 2. Afro-Americans—Biography—Juvenile
literature. 3. Educators—United States—Biography—Juvenile literature. 4. Tuskegee Institute—Juvenile
literature. [1. Washington, Booker T., 1856–1915. 2. Educators. 3. Afro-Americans—Biography.]
  I. McKissack, Fredrick. II. Title.
  E185.97.W4 M33 2001
  370'.92—dc21   00-010056

Printed in the United States of America

10 9 8 7 6 5 4 3 2 1

To Our Readers:
We have done our best to make sure all Internet addresses in this book were active and appropriate when we
went to press. However, the author and the publisher have no control over and assume no liability for the
material available on those Internet sites or on other Web sites they may link to. Any comments or suggestions
can be sent by e-mail to comments@enslow.com or to the address on the back cover.

Every effort has been made to locate all copyright holders of materials used in this book.
If any errors or omissions have occurred, corrections will be made in future editions of this book.

Illustration Credits: Frederick McKissack, pp. 22, 27B; Library of Congress, pp. 3, 4, 7, 8, 9, 11, 12, 13, 15, 16,
17, 20, 24; National Archives, p. 25; National Park Services, U.S. Department of the Interior, p. 6; Stamp Design
© U.S. Postal Services. Reproduced with permission. All rights reserved, p. 27T; Tuskegee University Archives,
pp. 19, 21, 26.

Cover Credits: Library of Congress; Frederick McKissack; National Park Services, U.S. Department of the
Interior; Tuskegee University Archives.

TABLE of CONTENTS

1 **From Slavery to Freedom** 5

2 **From Malden to Hampton** 10

3 **From Hampton to Tuskegee** 14

4 **The Tuskegee Dream** 18

5 **From Poverty to Fame** 23

Timeline 28

Words to Know 29

Learn More About
Booker T. Washington 31
  (Books and Internet Addresses)

Index 32

Booker Taliaferro Washington
1856–1915

CHAPTER 1

From Slavery to Freedom

Booker Taliaferro Washington never knew his birthday. He was born a slave, and the dates of slave births were not always written down. It is believed he was born sometime in 1856.

Booker and his family lived on a large Virginia plantation. His mother's name was Jane, and his stepfather was Washington Ferguson. Their one-room shack had a dirt floor. The door didn't shut well.

Booker was born in this log cabin in Virginia. Even young slave children were put to work. "There was no period of my life that was devoted to play," he said.

The windows had no glass. There were cracks in the walls.

Booker didn't even have a bed. He slept on the floor next to his brother John and his sister Amanda. A fireplace warmed the cabin. But it was always too hot or too cold in their home.

When Booker was five years old, his master put him to work. Booker fanned flies away from his master's table at mealtimes.

When he got older, he was given a new job. Every week he went to the mill with a load of corn. The corn was ground into meal there.

One day Booker passed by a school. He wanted to go inside. But slave children could not go to school. It was against the law!

This slave family lived in South Carolina in the mid-1800's. Booker said that his early years "were not very different from those of other slaves."

**With this document, President Lincoln
freed the slaves in the South.**

In 1861, the Civil War began. Northern and Southern states were at war with each other.

Lots of people wanted to end slavery. In 1863, President Abraham Lincoln freed all slaves in the South. But some slaves didn't know they were free until the war ended in 1865.

Northern soldiers came to the plantation where Booker and his family lived. The soldiers told them they were free. There was a lot of singing and shouting. Freedom had come at last!

Once they were free, many former slaves volunteered to fight in the Civil War on the side of the North.

CHAPTER 2

From Malden to Hampton

B ooker and his family were free. But life was not much better for them. They could not read or write. They had no money, no jobs, and no home. How would they live? What could they do?

Booker's stepfather moved to Malden, West Virginia, and sent for his family. He found a job at a salt furnace. At the furnace, salt was boiled out of water that came up from under the ground. Booker and his brother shoveled the salt into barrels.

Soon a school opened for black children in Malden. Booker finally got a chance to go to school.

The teacher asked him his name. He gave his first name, "Booker." The teacher wanted to know his last name. Booker did not know what to say. He had never had a last name. He thought about it. Then he told the teacher, "My name is Booker Washington."

Booker had to work in the coal mines, so he didn't go to school very often. But he read everything he could.

General Lewis Ruffner owned the salt furnace and coal mines in Malden. He hired Booker to do housework for his wife. Viola Ruffner was fussy and hard to please.

At the salt furnace, Booker's job was to shovel salt into barrels.

11

**After the Civil War, schools were started for African-Americans.
As a boy, Booker wished he could go to school.
"I had the feeling that to get into a schoolhouse . . . would be
the same as getting into paradise," he said.**

She wanted everything to be spotless. Booker did his best to please her.

Viola Ruffner liked Booker. So she let him read her books. She talked to him a lot about going to school.

Booker heard about a school in Hampton, Virginia. He wanted to go there. He worked even harder and saved his money. In the fall of 1872, Booker had enough money. He left Malden to go to Hampton Institute. The school was five hundred miles away. Booker walked in the rain. He slept on the ground. He hopped trains and begged for rides on the backs of wagons. It was a long, hard trip. But he would not turn back.

Booker was very eager to study at the Hampton Institute. He walked hundreds of miles to get there.

CHAPTER 3

From Hampton to Tuskegee

B ooker finally reached Hampton Institute. He was tired and dirty from traveling. He did not look like a student. Mary F. Mackie, the head teacher, told Booker there were no more openings. But then she told him to sweep a classroom floor. "Take the broom and sweep it," she said. She left Booker to do the job.

Viola Ruffner had taught Booker how to clean a room. He swept the classroom floor three times. Then he dusted it four times.

Mary Mackie came back later. She looked in the classroom and smiled. Then she decided to let him into the school. "I guess we will try you as a student," she said. Miss Mackie also hired Booker to be the janitor. And that is how he worked his way through school.

General Samuel C. Armstrong was the principal of Hampton. Most of the students who came to

These Hampton students are measuring the ground outside for their math class.

15

Booker later helped his brother John and sister Amanda go to school, too. John became a teacher.

Hampton had been slaves. General Armstrong believed that learning a skill like bricklaying or carpentry was the best way for African Americans to better themselves. Booker believed it, too.

Booker graduated from the Hampton Institute in 1875. He taught for a while in Malden and he studied for a year at a school in Washington, D.C. In 1879, General Armstrong asked Booker to come back to Hampton.

There, Booker helped teach the Native American students. He did the job very well.

16

Booker helped teach Native American students at Hampton. Here, one of the students talked to an American history class.

Booker was put in charge of the night school for adults by the end of the next year.

General Armstrong got a letter from a group of people in Tuskegee, Alabama. They needed a principal to help start a school. General Armstrong gave them Booker T. Washington's name. They offered Booker the job.

CHAPTER 4

The Tuskegee Dream

Booker reached Tuskegee in June 1881. He had lots of students. But he did not have a place to hold classes. He did not have any school supplies either.

That didn't stop Booker. He held his first class in a Tuskegee church on July 4, 1881. Thirty students came. Booker was the only teacher.

Six weeks passed. The school was still open. Booker hired Olivia Davidson to be his first teacher. She is often called the cofounder of

Tuskegee. She was in charge of all the women students. Everyone called her Miss D.

Three months after the school opened, some friends helped Booker buy an old farm. Booker, Miss D., and their students scrubbed and cleaned the buildings. Many people gave gifts for the school. Sometimes they gave money. Sometimes they gave food. Booker was happy to get any help he could.

Olivia Davidson, cofounder of Tuskegee, became Booker's second wife.

That is how Booker kept Tuskegee Institute open for a year. His work at Tuskegee became well known. Many people helped to make the Tuskegee dream come true. They gave their time and money.

Booker wanted Tuskegee to be a fine trade

school just like Hampton Institute. And it was. His students were learning how to lay brick, cut stone, hang a door, and make a suit. He liked to show visitors around Tuskegee. Most of the buildings were built by Tuskegee students and teachers. They also grew their own food at the Tuskegee farm.

Visitors to Tuskegee were often surprised to find the great educator working in his garden or feeding his chickens.

Booker was married three times. His first wife was his childhood friend Fannie Smith. They had one daughter, Portia.

Later, Fannie had a terrible fall. She died on May 4, 1884.

Booker married Miss D. a year later. They had two sons, Booker Jr. and Ernest Davidson. Olivia worked side by side with her husband Booker until she died on May 9, 1889.

A family portrait: Booker T. Washington, with third wife Margaret Murray, his daughter Portia, and his sons, Booker Jr. and Ernest Davidson.

Margaret Murray came to Tuskegee as a teacher. A year later, she was named the new principal for women students. In time she became Booker's third wife. They were married October 12, 1892. He was 36 years old and she was 31.

Carnegie Hall on the campus of Tuskegee University was built in 1901 by students and faculty.

CHAPTER 5

From Poverty to Fame

In the 1890s, African Americans were losing their right to vote. Unfair laws were being passed that took away many of their civil rights. Frederick Douglass, the most well-known black leader, died in 1895. People were wondering who would be the new black leader.

Booker gave a very important speech at the Atlanta Cotton Exposition on September 18, 1895. He said in his speech that the races could be as "separate as the fingers" on the hand in all social things. But when the country was in need (such as during war), the races could work together as one, like the fist.

Afterward, Booker T. Washington became the most powerful black leader of that time.

Many white people liked what Booker said.

Booker told his people to build their own houses so they would not be homeless; to grow food and raise animals so they would never be hungry.

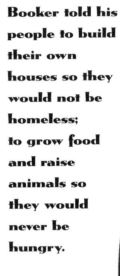

He was the leader they wanted. African Americans were divided. Some agreed with him. Others did not like his ideas. A lot of African Americans did not like white people telling them who their leaders should be.

Booker became a very powerful man. He talked with presidents and rich businessmen. In 1900, he started the National Negro Business League. The group tried to get more black businesses started.

Booker T. Washington was a very busy man, but he took time to write a book about his life. He called it *Up From Slavery*. He also enjoyed taking care of his garden, fishing,

Runaway slave Frederick Douglass was famous for speaking out to end slavery. He became an important African-American leader.

By 1906, Booker's sons, Ernest Davidson, left, and Booker Jr., were almost grown. Laura, Booker's adopted daughter, sits on his lap.

riding his horse, and telling visitors about the Tuskegee dream.

During a trip to New York, Booker became sick. Margaret went to bring him home. Booker T. Washington died a few hours after he got home to Alabama on November 14, 1915.

In 1940, the U.S. Postal Service issued a stamp honoring Booker T. Washington.

This well-known statue is on the campus of Tuskegee University. Booker T. Washington is shown "lifting the veil of ignorance from his people."

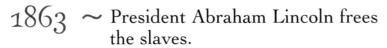

timeLiNe

1872

1856 ~ Born a slave in Virginia.

1863 ~ President Abraham Lincoln frees
the slaves.

1865 ~ Family moves to Malden, West Virginia.

1872 ~ Enters Hampton Institute in Hampton,
Virginia.

1875 ~ Graduates from Hampton Institute;
takes teaching job in Malden.

1879 ~ Returns to Hampton to teach.

1881 ~ Starts Tuskegee Institute in an old
empty church.

1895 ~ Gives speech at the Atlanta Cotton Exposition.

1895

1900 ~ Starts the National Negro Business League.

1901 ~ Writes autobiography, *Up From Slavery*.

1915 ~ Dies November 14.

Words to Know

Atlanta Cotton Exposition—A large business and industry fair held in 1895. The South wanted to show how much progress it had made since the Civil War.

businessman—A person who earns money by selling a product or giving a service. Booker T. Washington wanted more black people to start businesses.

civil war—A war fought within a country. The United States Civil War was fought between northern and southern states from 1861 to 1865.

Douglass, Frederick—A black leader who worked to end slavery. He died in 1895. Booker T. Washington took his place as the most important black leader in America at that time.

graduate—To finish a course of study at a school.

institute—a place of learning; a school.

janitor—A person who keeps a building clean. Booker worked his way through school as a janitor.

National Negro Business League—A group that was started by Booker T. Washington to help African Americans open more businesses.

WORDS TO KNOW

plantation—A large farm. When Booker was born, many slaves worked in the fields at plantations.

president—The leader of a country or a group.

principal—The head of a school. Booker was the principal of Tuskegee Institute.

salt furnace—A place where salt was boiled out of water brought up from underground. The salt was put into large barrels to be sold.

slave—A person who is owned by another person and forced to work for no pay.

trade school—A school where students learn how to be skilled craftsmen, such as carpenters, bricklayers, tailors, and printers.

Learn more about Booker T. Washington

Books

Amper, Thomas. *Booker T. Washington*. Minneapolis, Minn.: Lerner Publishing Group, 1998.

Gleiter, Jan. *Booker T. Washington*. Austin, Tex.: Raintree Steck-Vaughn Publishers, 1995.

McLoone, Margo. *Booker T. Washington*. Mankato, Minn.: Capstone Press, Inc., 1997.

Internet Addresses

The African American Journey: Booker T. Washington
<http://www.worldbook.com/fun/aajourny/html/bh065.html>

Legends of Tuskegee
Click on Booker T. Washington to learn more about his life through words and pictures.
<http://www.cr.nps.gov/csd/exhibits/tuskegee/index.htm>

index

a

African Americans,
rights of, 23–24
Armstrong, General
Samuel C., 15–16,
17
Atlanta Cotton
Exposition, 23–24

c

Civil War, 9

d

Douglass, Frederick,
23, 25

e

Emancipation
Proclamation, 8

H

Hampton Institute,
13–17, 20
Native American
students at, 16–17

L

Lincoln, President
Abraham, 8, 9

m

Mackie, Mary F., 14–15
Malden, West Virginia,
10–11, 13, 16

Miss D. *See* Washington,
Olivia Davidson

N

National Negro
Business League, 25
New York, 27

R

Ruffner, General Lewis,
11
Ruffner, Viola, 11, 14

S

salt furnace, 10, 11
slavery, 5–9

t

Tuskegee, Alabama, 17,
18–19
Tuskegee Institute,
17–20, 22

u

Up From Slavery, 25

v

Virginia, 5, 6

w

Washington, Booker
Taliaferro
birth of, 5, 6

brother and sister
of, 6, 10, 16
children of, 20–21, 26
death of, 27
education, 12, 14–16
founds Tuskegee
Institute, 18
freed from slavery, 9
marriages of, 20–22
parents of, 5, 10
Washington, Booker T.,
Jr. (son), 21, 26
Washington, D.C., 16
Washington, Ernest
Davidson (son), 21,
26
Washington, Fannie
Smith (first wife),
20–21
Washington, Laura
(adopted daughter),
26
Washington, Margaret
Murray (third
wife), 21, 22
Washington, Olivia
Davidson "Miss D."
(second wife),
18–19, 21
Washington, Portia
(daughter), 20, 21